The Wind In My Face

Chandranil Das Gupta

BookLeaf Publishing

India | USA | UK

Presentation by *BookLeaf Publishing*

Web: www.bookleafpub.com

E-mail: info@bookleafpub.com

ISBN: 9789363311619

First edition 2024

DEDICATION

This book is dedicated to my mother Jayanti Das Gupta, and my sister Rupa Gupta (a well known author), both of whom always wanted to see my name on a book cover, but which never came to pass. My mother departed this world in May 2024, and my sister in November 2022

Too little, too late; the endless sad litany of "If only …"

ACKNOWLEDGEMENT

My thanks for this work goes to the prime mover behind my participation in the #TheWriteAngle Challenge, my daughter Aeshna, who made me aware of this challenge and facilitated my participation and subsequently joined my wife Ruma and son Adwitya as my enthusiastic cheerleaders right up to completion of this little book.

PREFACE

This is my first book of poems, indeed my first book! Its unexpected birth is entirely due to BookLeaf Publishing's #TheWriteAngle 21 day/21 poem challenge, which I responded to with considerable trepidation mixed with the lure of a challenge which one has not encountered before. So it was then that I jumped off the springboard into the unfamiliar waters of poetry, with a helpful push from my loved ones.

As a first effort, I have tried to keep it simple and have written about things that I care about or intrigue me. I enjoyed the experience of writing poetry enormously and hope it will connect with the readers through shared feelings, emotions and a sense of wonder.

P.S: All the characters mentioned in this book are entirely fictional.

Forced Tower Entry

I stand before a doorway,

Covered with creepers,

Through dark passages,

A great creaky door

opens reluctantly,

To let me in,

A flood of foggy light;

Angry upset people;

In vaporous shadows,

Glare at me.

"Who let him in?

Into this hallowed Babel,

Of elephantine tusks and

textured incomprehensibility?"

"the back door!" shrieked one;

" a cat burglar!" says another

"Looking for our secret elixir

That entwines in love

or marches off to war,

At our beck and call"

Says the bald poetic one:

"Tainted by the world without,

Uncomprehending this lout;

Of thousand-eyed equinox,

(vision he doubtless mocks),

or of the sceptred orb of time,

Bereft he's of meter or rhyme.

So let poetic invectives rain,

Roaring to evict the profane.

Literary skills so very sparse

Kick him quickly on the arse!"

Truth catches up fast.

Into outer darkness cast;

With inspiration forlorn

It's lonely in Babble-on.

The Brick

Vice-grip the writer's block,

So the brick I contemplate,

How came I upon this rock?

Fruitlessly laboured till late.

Why are bricks so fire red?

In quiet desperation I asked.

'From iron,' my mind dredged.

"Whence the iron," I persisted.

The celestial furnace in the star

Smelts atoms in its fiery womb

Creating starlight seen from far.

Ceaseless stoking is star's tomb;

Fertilising birth of destroyer iron;

Its nascent cradle quenches light;

Star's fate is most terribly forlorn.

Destroyed the star's shining might.

Space and time curve and bend,

Starstuff hurtles in at speed of light,

Speeding fire's journey at centre ends.

A titanic explosion intensely bright!

What could it for future life portend?

Over Universe spewed, iron and all;

Everything to paint future's canvas.

Cosmically dispersed by the fireball,

Creating air, plants, bricks and us.

I take out the brick from a broken wall

and sit with it under a spreading tree.

Absolution granted now of every sin;

Now the earth, tree, clay and me,

journey as inseparably eternal kin.

Apparition

Flying as a streak of blur,

It set my heart quite astir.

Braking to a full dead-stop;

Within silence of a pin drop.

In the scabbard of red flower,

a sheathed sword-beak hover.

It drinks deep of nectar store,

Until it cannot hold any more.

Metallic sheen of its plumage,

Glitters in summery sun's rage.

As Nature's fortune fast depress,

Birds are becoming less and less.

Sparrows are gone, ditto the crows;

With pitiless humans, nothing grows.

So startled was I by this apparition,

A fugitive bird from a royal mansion.

Could it be a hummingbird sublime,

That flew in from some distant clime?

Or this blazing summer most unkind,

Created some figment in my mind?

Annoying Fly

Looks like it's going to be a race.

Thinking so, I step up the pace.

So intent it is to sit on my head,

This blasted fly I quite dread.

A vermin that is really louche,

Waits patiently for the ambush.

As on my morning walk I start;

Flying at my face I see it dart.

The fly that was just sitting on rotten rind,

Is now racing me backward against the wind.

As if it has guessed my hopeless intent,

Never seen a creature with mind so bent.

To teach a lesson my weakness it mocks;

"Apex creature, huh? Now walk the talk!"

The Keeper

A childhood friend known for long,

To the sky and earth does belong.

Counter of stars in the firmament,

Seer of raindrops from heaven sent,

Perfection checker of rainbow's arc;

Sleuth of cruelly stripped tree bark;

For the doting strays provisions he stacks;

Checks celestial dome for leaks or cracks.

Bemused everyone for many a summer.

Marches he on to a different drummer.

Every bit of information he keeps abreast,

From the shoveler duck to a neural crest.

No one has seen him reading in his lair;

guess he plucks knowledge from the air.

So unconstrained by time or place is he;

 "Tell me, can monkeys underwater see?"

This to old ladies in their noontime nap

Shriek when they spy him in curtains' gap;

Not realising the strange man so bold,

Beats within him a pure heart of gold.

The Fish Vendor

Like a sonic boom from afar,

Her rising cry does quite jar.

Ingratiating cats pad in line,

For bits of fish they do pine.

Her old basket she does fill,

Fishes that flop or quite still.

Sweat and ice water mingle,

On her body old and single.

Careworn face's not beaten;

Since morning has not eaten.

Damp sari starts to bedraggle,

Tucked, she's ready to haggle.

So very practised is her art,

Customers with money part

With passing of every year,

Her fish basket gets heavier.

The stair's climb takes longer,

She isn't getting any younger.

Spurred onwards by dignity;

From dependence to being free.

One day may be a reckoning;

Swing of ancient scales bring,

In shadows edge a cadence,

Bursting light of providence.

Heavier Than Air

To convince myself I indeed try,

That pressurised tubes can fly.

Though it is a machine of Rube,

Maniacal spinning with the lube,

Revving engines on the wing,

No comfort to knuckle bring.

Ungainly trundle down taxi track,

Wings waggle so, they may crack.

Snaking wires and gizmos concealed,

Ultimately to the cockpit controls lead.

Pilot pushes clenched throttle forward,

Rattle-jolts like a stampede hard;

experience that will find no bard.

Nose up wheelies for a while;

Gravity challenges air's guile.

Old Bernoulli wins by a mile,

Aluminium tube flies in style.

When safely in the air I think,

The tech marvel in does sink.

Elevators, flaps and ailerons,

Moved by the flowing electron.

Control surfaces' dancing goal,

Lets planes twist, rock and roll.

Tons of metal move and shift,

Creating the swift upward lift.

Exquisite timing and precision;

Myriad devices hum in unison.

Each depending on the other;

With one's glitch, others falter.

Each part by someone built;

Has fulfilled specs to the hilt.

Each fuel pump delivers PSI;

Less or more and people die.

Fuel to engine's fiery ring goes,

Engines RPM precise, no woes.

Pilot sets flaps at ten degrees;

Servos, gears and chips agree

To work together in harmony.

Promises by many so well kept,

Metal at flight becomes adept.

In a world where it's a rarity,

Gravity's defied by integrity.

Grande Corporate

Yell, shout, intimidate and stand tall,

Failure strikes, weaklings take the fall.

Ceaselessly scold, take away dignity,

From criticism you will have immunity.

Fear in mind, no one'll have impunity.

Mirror should never show you as you,

Banish all that's inconveniently true.

Never let others see as you really are,

Image is everything, worship from far.

As feedback loops breaks and shatters,

Divine infallibility is what really matters.

Psychic energy false mirror wants more

and more, but there is little left in store.

Summon up the grand vision,

Objections are high treason,

When things go wrong and there's fuss,

Look for suckers to throw under the bus.

With energy and credibility gone,

Fate awaits that's mostly forlorn.

Finally the sands of time runs out,

None care for your shriek or shout.

Shattered career's strewn around,

Shifts under feet the firm ground.

Shareholders' panic and stampede;

Nothing can the pent-up fury impede.

Share prices fall off a steep cliff;

Soon comes the arrival of bailiff.

Court spurns prayer for bail;

So it's now a long time in jail.

Finally out, the shadows loom;

Forsaken till the crack of doom.

Wife's gone, children do not call;

Someone to only himself gave all.

Recounts days of imagined glory;

Time drips slowly till end of story.

Liar's Pyre

As the world builds truth's pyres,

Instead it should be for the liars.

Like Pinocchio in lies' deep mire;

His nose's length grew more dire.

As falsehoods grow ever higher,

Liars should have noses on fire.

Truth's not just philosophy's vision,

But it is the deepest root of reason.

Truth lies at the heart of all cultures;

Eternal and not the feast of vultures.

'Satyamev Jayate' is the tallest tree,

'Know the truth and it shall set you free'.

Truth drives all tech and science;

All invention and intellectual licence.

The mobile you hold, your identity,

To tech owes its miraculous utility.

Homes you build, the planes you fly,

Impossible, if we lived in a sea of lies.

It is the lie with which everyday ends,

Gathering Dark Age's gloom descends

The truth-tellers I'll greatly admire,

Won't fall prey to the value buyers.

Ones who will admit their mistakes;

Character's courage is all it takes.

Who no flattery of friends expects;

Nor sees enemies' barbs as threats.

But the bitter beneficial truth begets.

So evolution progresses day by day;

Metamorphosed butterfly flies away!

Wind on my Face - Runtime

When young, for no reason would I race,

Just to feel the blowing wind on my face.

So a silent, solitary runner did I become,

And felt the heartbeats and blood hum.

Up was I everyday before break of dawn,

Well before dewdrops dried on the lawn.

Off was I running, an unremarkable pace;

Just to feel the morning wind on my face.

Ran in the rain and the thunderstorms too,

Crackling lightning bolts, excitement brew.

Bewildered wonder if my senses did I lose,

To run in driving rain in squelching shoes.

I stop not, no, not even to tighten the lace,

Fleeing leaves and errant wind on my face.

Good things must inevitably one day end,

Who knows what the future will portend?

Wind On My Face - The Doctor

The doc tut-tutted and pressed my knee,

Pinching harder, "Does it hurt?" asked he.

Was the doctor joking? My agonised yell,

Must have sent all bats fleeing from hell!

Flexed, poked, prodded taking his time,

Gave his judgement like judge sublime.

"Wore away cartilage when you did run.

Must know your running days are done"

Heard voices say from depths of my soul,

"Can't go down; with the punch will I roll"

Imploring, pleading to change his mind

In his stoic silence, doc was most unkind.

"No one," I told him "can break my will."

He scribbled and said, "Here's your bill."

Wind On My Face - Dark Knight

Listless days of not running took its toll,

That turned into dark nights of the soul.

The faint air-buffet of a runner going by,

Lashed me like a tornado ripping the sky.

When in a corner expect gloom to attack;

Or find ways to make corners' axes crack.

Resolved to fight on, not give in with grace;

For the faintest chance of wind on my face.

Wind On My Face - Full Cycle

Self-confined was I, as if I had sinned,

Walls are the sworn enemy of the wind.

I grieved that in a life quite far from late,

I was walking with quite a stumbling gait.

Would best part of life round this revolve?

Get up! No choice now left but to evolve.

Getting my weight down, 10x the benefit.

Until I could into my old small clothes fit.

On the bicycle before cock crow at dawn.

The nightbirds to home still had not flown.

Time when dreams and wakefulness share,

My wheels were singing in cool morning air.

Strengthen the body especially the legs;

Give up forever the seductive spirit pegs.

Exercise, weights, pushups, painful squat;

An iron cage around body and legs begot.

From the double replacement of the knee,

Forever, I am hopeful now of being set free.

I still can't run, but on my bicycle I do race.

Life regained, streaming wind on my face!

Friend and Unicorn

My friend who was a carefree soul like me,

Bright and brilliant scholar's mind had he.

Everything was fine until terrible fate befell,

Mind sank into darkness of deep, dark well.

Electrodes on head delivered mighty jolts.

Mind broke away under hammering volts.

A few pieces reassembled, most were lost.

Normality's faint semblance at high cost.

Reduced to a skeleton in baggy clothes,

He wandered distraught on open roads.

Halting speech couched rambling thought,

That meant not many his company sought.

Forced by loneliness that would try a saint,

He turned to his brush and tubes of paint.

One day when he came for his cup of tea,

 A canvas he placed on my mother's knee.

That day he left without saying a word,

The tea leaves still brewing unpoured.

The painting showed a Unicorn surprising;

Bloodied hindquarters in flames fast rising.

But skyward was its head, wings unfurled,

Its thick white mane was beautifully curled.

Its noble visage tranquil, seeing the light,

Skyward it headed, into starry, starry night.

From that day on he got better and better,

He went back to being a man of the letter.

He plucked knowledge from the very air,

Wafting as vagrant breezes into his lair.

Brimful questions or discovery of the day,

Pondered we around the convivial tea tray.

No longer was he headed for dark eternity,

Returned to a mortal pasture of fraternity!

The Lake

Girded by mighty trees of commanding height;

Tranquil the lake reflecting morning light.

My companions liked it but not impressed.

"There are few others like it," they stressed.

'Twas difficult to explain to them, I didn't try;

Difference is seeing with your mind or eye.

Many years ago a man lived on this shore,

Who came here to find life's hidden core.

He put away books, forsook possessions

Read the book of life and learnt its lessons.

Seasons changed as Earth circled the Sun;

Wisdom he gained as time's sands did run.

In the cabin he built with his own hands,

Great words penned reached many lands.

Bridging time they made philosophy sing;

Listened intently Gandhi, Mandela and King.

Many glorious changes did they bring,

And mankind's moral transformation ring.

All this from ring of water and hermit's hut;

Shaking abject stupor, lifting from deep rut.

His words find their mark like a true arrow;

A philosophy that's sublime and so thorough!

Chimpy's Look

Chimpy was a dog, russet and white stray.

Who renewed acquaintanceship every day.

Although strong and street-smart was he,

Wise, he always knew when to just let it be.

Unlike other canines he never chased a cat,

In fact, they often curled up on the doormat.

Welcome wherever he wandered in the town,

Ate what was given but never wolfed it down.

Patiently he would wait for me to throw a stick,

If I was preoccupied he would give me a lick.

One day he crept under my bed and puked;

Against house rules; him I sternly rebuked.

Gave me a sad look and slunk off into the night,

Did not return tho' 'twas well past morning
light.

Cook I sent to fetch him and set things right.

He came back, "Dead," he said, "of snakebite."

I will never ever forget Chimpy's last sad look;

I can only lay it down gently in this little book.

Like fishbone stuck in soul's throat 'twill lie,

Helpless I am to sin atone until the day I die.

Colliding Ages of Creation and Destruction

Our distant ancestors looked up at starry sky,

Their thoughts would soar to the most high.

To give answers and calm their deepest fear,

"Who am I? From where? What am I doing here?"

Ages came and went over thousands of years,

Eons of stone, fire, metal mute witness bears.

Thousands of years was width of an Age's span;

Plenty of time to adjust, evolve and ahead plan.

But come 1900 things begin hurtling at
light-speed;

Einstein of Relativity made a great unicorn
steed.

Equations of clock-time not of constant flow,

Time could speed or even stop or become slow.

Also from the equations fell out a mighty seed,

Of nuclear destruction or endless energy breed.

The First Age Nuclear, a nightmare of dread;

People wondered about incineration in bed.

Even as reactors lighted up millions of homes,

Dreams of limitless, clean fusion energy in
tomes.

Nuclear Age starts but no time for breath to
catch,

Space Age is upon us and beginning to hatch.

The Sputnik soars and Yuri Gagarin orbits Earth;

Neil on Moon stands, Man leaves cradle of birth.

Military satellites gird the Earth hinting of
StarWar,

Everything's hair trigger, maybe we're done for.

Two mighty Ages to adjust to, fun has just
begun,

Computer Age comes careening jumping the
gun.

It's now about bytes, chips and processing brute,

Now even the most reluctant Luddite can
compute.

But in darkened rooms hooded spectres fashion,

Malware and hacking that can bring down a
nation.

Struggling with Three Ages but far from done,

The Biotechnological Age has begun its run.

Giving Man for first time the power of a creator,

Artificial life is first created in a climatic theatre.

Unleashing the promise of curatives wondrous,

Existential threats unleashed by demonic virus.

Burden of four ages oppress, weight of many a tonne;

Meteor-strike AI Age usurps man's place in the Sun.

Alt reality, music, art created at wave of a wand;

Man's destiny shrinks from mighty ocean to pond.

As the populace over AI's fantastic feats rave,

Looms gloomy prospect of Man as abject slave.

Struggling like Atlas under mounting orbs of Ages;

What does not break can make, say the sages.

Is it a great mental leap we need to make?

Darwin's choking hold to decisively break?

Are we confronting a great evolutionary stage?

Is it time for Man to turn and write a new page?

We Should Not Be Here

Science says there is no reason for us to be here;

This cosmic luck makes life ever more dear.

Fashioned in the crucible of impossible event,

It almost seems the Universe for man was
meant.

If so many parameters had deviated by a hair,

It's very clear indeed that Man wouldn't be
there.

The Big Bang started from a point infinitely hot;

All that formed therefrom which before was not.

Mighty battle ensued 'tween substance and light,

Universe's fate hung on outcome of the fight.

At long last, substance prevailed and light lost,

Matter's victory came at a very great cost.

Light receded and its shining rays were lost

Life's bricks laid but the Universe turned dark.

How could life begin without light's vital spark?

For aeons, atoms roamed Universe quite
aimlessly,

Until pulled together in great clouds by gravity.

Gravity's iron grip formed spiral whirlpool
knots,

That kindled latent nuclear fires intensely hot.

Thus stars were born, their bursting rays,

Ended darkness's long reign, kept it at bay.

Planets formed around many a star,

Orbiting, some nearby and others far.

Life would in time establish its might,

Man could now silently step into light!

Sensuous

The baby's fist closing on a finger,

Flower scents on East wind linger.

Melody soars up to realm unheard,

Turquoise flash of a Kingfisher bird.

Blinding light and lightning's crash;

Driving rain on windowpanes dash;

Soothing waves after a bracing run;

Bumble bees weave in summer sun;

Carpets under flower-dripping trees;

Faint song borne on a gypsy breeze;

Parchment skin on old woman's face,

Darjeeling tea brews on cotton lace;

Shout of lost long remembered voice;

Wonder of once-in-a-lifetime choice;

Crystal stars singing in the winter sky;

Old photos; memories of days gone by;

First leaf of autumn drifts onto the lap;

Country seen that was only on the map;

First coming of age, drink with old dad;

Impossible team win, world goes mad;

Wisp of hair blows on beloved's brow;

Splashes as on the tranquil lake I row,

Lying down at night on drifting boat,

On whirling sky does Milky Way float.

Wisdom transcends time and space,

Like heaven's cool wind on my face.

The gust holds its boisterous sway,

Pages that were written blow away.

Universe Arises

The universe is of abundant energy made,

luminous light and ghostly particles inlaid.

Questing the Cosmos we are sensing,

By sight, taste, smell, touch, hearing.

Our eyes, ears, nerves just empty props,

Until tiny drips of energy on them drops.

Then magic happens, Universe does Arise;

For each energy drop has to its origin ties.

(Scientists are adept at names that turn on,

They call the light-speed energy drops 'photon').

When photon's journey on our eyes end,

Picture of pulses' origin to mind send.

Origin may be of flowers, star or friend.

Harder the rain of photons from source
originate,

The sharper the image the mind does create.

Shocking idea follows, bit hard to resist,

Consciousness makes the Universe exist!

Prayer For Nothing More

Every person is of chain of miracles born;

Marvels from Old Time's book pages torn.

Magic distilled from quantum-spacetime,

Tiniest to largest scales, difficult to rhyme.

Everything has conspired to make possible life;

Four great forces that shape evolution's strife.

Like all things in the very beginning were one,

In the simple Universe that had only just begun.

Forces flew apart as the Universe crystallised,

In their deepest essence, what is most prized,

Their qualities are exactly as needed for life,

Life balances on the edge of a sharp knife.

This is miracle enough, but that's far from all,

So many strange coincidences into place fall.

A myriad happenstances, far too many to recall,

Which when narrated would be like a story tall.

If any of these odd happenings were bit
different,

No life at all in this Universe would be present

SETI sends cosmic messages, opens giant eye

Years and years pass by, but there is no reply.

Is life on Earth the miracle to all miracles end?

Life is made commonplace or so we like to
pretend.

Contempt born of familiarity, life becomes
cheap.

We falter and fail to make evolution's giant leap.

So astonishingly fortunate are we to possess,

The life fire that burns within our sacred recess.

So no need to implore the heavens for more,

The munificent Universe has given all in its
store.

So it's time now to justify cosmic gift supreme,

By bringing to reality what was a distant dream!

www.ingramcontent.com/pod-product-compliance
Lightning Source LLC
La Vergne TN
LVHW021241200726
843509LV00012B/1556